LIFE SCIENCE

You and Your Genes

REBECCA L. JOHNSON

PICTURE CREDITS

Cover: Grant V. Faint/gettyimages. Page 1 Dennis Hallinan/gettyimages; pages 2–3 Bob Torrez/gettyimages; page 4 Ron Kimball Photography; page 6 Wally McNamee/CORBIS; page 7 Eric Risberg/AP; page 8 © L. Willatt/SPL/Photo Researchers, Inc.; pages 8–9 art by Stephen R. Wagner; pages 11 (left), 13 (#1 top) David Young-Wolff/PhotoEdit; pages 11 (right), 13 (#2 top) Michael Newman/PhotoEdit; pages 11 (low), 15 (low), 23 (right) PhotoDisc®; page 12 Digital Vision; page 13 (#3 top) Stephen Simpson/gettyimages; page 13 (#4 top) Spencer Grant III/Stock Boston/PictureQuest; page 13 (#1 low) Norbert Schafer/Corbis Stock Market; pages 13 (#2 low), 28 Lloyd Wolf; page 13 (#3 low) Dan McCoy/Rainbow; page 13 (#4 low) Dan Kline/Visuals Unlimited; pages 14, 23 (left) The Granger Collection; page 15 (top) © Biophoto Associates/Science Source/Photo Researchers, Inc.; page 16 (left) © SPL/Photo Researchers, Inc.; page 16 (right) © A. Barrington Brown/Science Source/Photo Researchers, Inc.; pages 16–17 © Dorling Kindersley; page 18 James L. Stanfield/NGS Image Collection; page 20 © David Parker/SPL/Photo Researchers, Inc.; page 21 © David M. Phillips/Photo Researchers, Inc.; page 22 Ron Edmonds/AP; page 24 © Reuters NewMedia Inc./CORBIS; page 25 Ted Horowitz/Corbis Stock Market; page 26 © Dennis Degnan/CORBIS; page 27 (left) Jose Luis Pelaez Inc./Corbis Stock Market; page 27 (right) courtesy Howard University; pages 28, 29 Precision Graphics; page 30 Eurelios/Phototake.

Produced through the worldwide resources of the National Geographic Society, John M. Fahey, Jr., President and Chief Executive Officer; Gilbert M. Grosvenor, Chairman of the Board; Nina D. Hoffman, Executive Vice President and President, Books and School Publishing.

PREPARED BY NATIONAL GEOGRAPHIC SCHOOL PUBLISHING
Ericka Markman, Senior Vice President; Steve Mico, Editorial Director; Barbara Seeber, Editorial Manager; Lynda McMurray, Amy Sarver, Project Editors; Roger B. Hirschland, Consulting Editor; Jim Hiscott, Design Manager; Karen Thompson, Art Director; Kristin Hanneman, Illustrations Manager; Diana Bourdrez, Tom DiGiovanni, Ruth Goldberg, Photo Editors; Christine Higgins, Photo Coordinator; Matt Wascavage, Manager of Publishing Services; Sean Philpotts, Production Coordinator.

Production: Clifton M. Brown III, Manufacturing and Quality Control.

CONSULTANT/REVIEWER
Dr. Irwin Slesnick, Professor of Biology, Western Washington University, Bellingham, Washington

PROGRAM DEVELOPMENT
Kate Boehm Jerome

BOOK DESIGN
3r1 Group

Published by the National Geographic Society
Washington, D.C. 20036-4688

Product No. 4J41260

ISBN-13: 978-0-7922-8866-4
ISBN-10: 0-7922-8866-1

Printed in Canada.

11
10 9 8 7

Cover photo: DNA double helix

Contents

Gene Power

Animal watching at the zoo is a great way to spend an afternoon. There's a mother tiger and her brand new cubs. Wait a minute—one of the cubs has white instead of orange fur. How can that be?

In every other way, the white tiger looks like tigers are supposed to look. It has black stripes, big paws with sharp claws, and a long tail. So what's the secret to its snow-colored fur? Its fur is white, rather than orange, because of a difference in a single gene.

Genes are tiny structures inside cells that control the way cells grow and change. Genes are like a set of instructions for building living organisms and keeping them functioning properly. Whether it's a tiger or a toadstool, the cells of every living thing contain genes. And that includes you. Your genes are mostly responsible for how you look, from the color of your hair to the fact that you don't have a tail. It's true that your **environment** influences how you look and act. But genes play a big role.

Genes are tiny. Yet they are powerful. They must be, if just one gene can make the difference between an orange tiger and a white one. In this book you'll explore what we have learned about genes. You'll also learn what scientists are still trying to find out about these mysterious little structures in our cells.

Chapter 1

Life's Little Instruction Book

Tiger Woods's are attached. Tara Lipinski's definitely are not. What are we talking about? Earlobes—those soft little bits of flesh at the bottom of a person's ears.

1998 Olympic figure skating medalists Michelle Kwan, Tara Lipinski, and Lu Chen

Notice how Tiger's earlobes are attached to the side of his head. But Tara's are detached. Her earlobes hang free. Which type of earlobe do you have—attached or detached? Grab a mirror and check it out.

Like the color of a tiger's fur, the shape of your earlobes is caused by a difference in a single gene. Earlobe shape is a human characteristic, or **trait**. We each have thousands of genes that control thousands of different traits. The instructions for some traits, like earlobe shape, are found in just one gene. Other traits are the result of many genes acting together.

Has anyone ever said to you, "You have your mother's smile" or "your father's nose"? You have many traits that are very similar to your parents' traits because you **inherited** your genes from them. Half of your genes came from your mother, and half came from your father. Those genes all came together in the cell that eventually developed into you.

The set of genes that you inherited—your own personal set of instructions for life—are unique. Unless you have an identical twin, there is no one else on Earth exactly like you.

Even though identical twins are the same genetically, why might they look somewhat different from each other?

Golf champion Tiger Woods

In Search of Genes

Where are these genes that control so much of what makes you *you?* They're inside almost every cell in your body.

If you looked at one of your cells—say, a skin cell from the tip of your finger—under a microscope, you'd notice a dark blob near the center. That's the cell's **nucleus**. Inside the nucleus are long strands that are coiled up like tiny springs. These strands are your **chromosomes**.

There are 46 chromosomes, or 23 pairs, in each cell body. One member of each pair came from your mother. The other member of each pair came from your father.

Each of your chromosomes is made up of a substance called **DNA**, which stands for deoxyribonucleic acid. Scientists know that DNA looks a bit like a spiral staircase.

Now, at last, we've found the location of the genes. A gene is a particular length of DNA, a specific section of the spiral staircase that coils into chromosomes that lie in the nucleus deep within each cell.

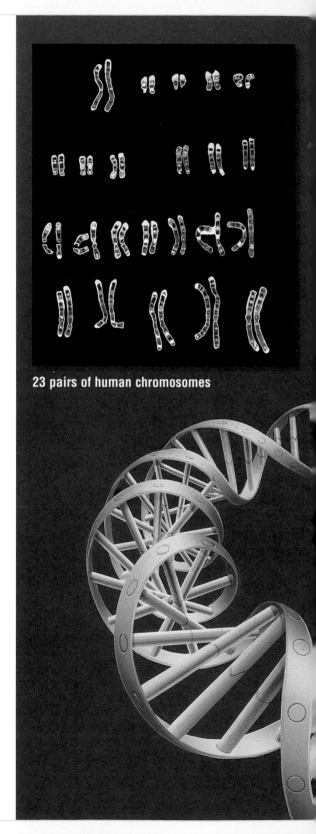

23 pairs of human chromosomes

Chromosomes

Nucleus of cell

DNA strand

Interesting Questions ... I.Q.

Q: Are genes found in *every* cell of a person's body?

A: No. Genes are in every cell except red blood cells. Red blood cells lose their nuclei—and thus their chromosomes—soon after they are formed. That's why red blood cells are shaped a bit like doughnuts—the squished-in part in the center is where the nucleus once was.

Q: Does every human cell with a nucleus contain 23 pairs of chromosomes?

A: No. All cells with a nucleus except the reproductive cells, which are called eggs and sperm, have 23 pairs of chromosomes. Each egg and sperm cell contains just 23 individual chromosomes, not 23 pairs. When an egg and a sperm join, the resulting cell—that can eventually develop into a new person—has 23 pairs, or 46 chromosomes.

Working in Pairs

Remember the examples of tiger fur color and earlobe shape? A single gene controls each of these traits. Actually, they're controlled by a single pair of genes. That's because people (and tigers) inherit pairs of chromosomes, and therefore pairs of genes, from their parents. This means that for each gene on one member of a chromosome pair, there's a similar gene in the same place on the other member of that chromosome pair.

How do these pairs of genes control a trait like earlobe shape? Well, the two genes for this trait that you inherited—one from each of your parents—may be different. Most genes come in slightly different forms, called **alleles**. Different alleles are instructions for slightly different versions of the same trait.

Two alleles are involved in earlobe shape. One is the **dominant** allele, and it calls for detached earlobes. The other is the **recessive** allele, which calls for attached earlobes. The dominant allele gets its name from the fact that it can override or cover up the recessive allele.

How does this work in you and other people? If you inherited two dominant alleles for earlobe shape —one from each of your parents— you have detached earlobes. If you inherited one dominant allele and one recessive allele, you still have detached earlobes because the dominant allele overrode the recessive one. However, if you inherited two copies of the recessive form of the gene for earlobe shape, your lobes are attached.

What traits have you inherited from your parents?

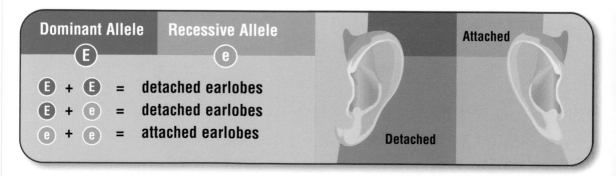

Dominant Allele	Recessive Allele		
E	e		
E + E	=	detached earlobes	
E + e	=	detached earlobes	
e + e	=	attached earlobes	

Attached

Detached

Blue eyes

Brown eyes

Complicating Factors

If all traits were controlled by single pairs of genes, then **genetics**, the study of how traits are inherited, would be easy. However, it turns out to be very complicated.

Many traits are controlled by more than a single pair of genes. The color of your eyes, for example, is the result of many pairs of genes working together in not very clear-cut ways. This fact makes it more difficult to figure out the job of each gene.

It's true that genes play a major role in determining how an organism looks and functions. However, genes aren't the only influence. Environmental factors shape living things too.

Take Siamese cats for instance. Genes contain instructions for the color of their fur. Yet temperature also can affect their fur color. Where a Siamese cat's body is warmest, its fur is light in color. On slightly cooler parts of the cat, like its ears, paws, nose, and tail, the fur grows in darker.

Now think about your own body. Your genes are responsible for the fact that you have muscles in your arms and legs. However, you can make your muscles bigger and stronger by exercising. Things you do and experiences you have—together with instructions given by your genes—shape you into a unique person.

Picture This

Tracking Down Traits

These two pages show human traits that **geneticists** know are controlled by a single pair of genes. In each set of photos below, the top photo shows the trait that results if a person inherits one or two of the dominant alleles for that trait. Which form of each of these traits do you have?

DOMINANT TRAIT

RECESSIVE TRAIT

① Tongue-rolling

The student above is able to roll her tongue because she inherited one or two copies of the dominant allele for this trait. If you don't have the dominant allele, you can't do the roll.

② Long Eyelashes

The length of your eyelashes is another gene-controlled trait. Cosmetics can make eyelashes look longer, but their effect is temporary.

③ Widow's Peak

A widow's peak or point in your hairline is another distinctive genetic trait. If you have a widow's peak, do other members of your family have one too?

④ Hitchhiker's Thumb

A single pair of genes controls whether or not you can bend the top joint of your thumb at a backward angle to the bottom joint (lower photo).

Solving a Mystery

Sherlock Holmes, the famous English detective, pulled out his magnifying glass. He peered at the wall through the glass. Aha! A single fingerprint. It was the clue that would solve the case!

The fictional character
Sherlock Holmes

The Sherlock Holmes stories are some of the most popular detective stories of all time. Holmes solved cases that stumped everyone else. Yet scientists who study genes and how they work have been trying to solve a mystery that's far more complicated than any case Holmes ever took on.

In the 1950s scientists achieved major breakthroughs in the "Case of the Inherited Traits." By then, geneticists had discovered DNA and figured out that it is made up of chemical building blocks called **nucleotides**. Each nucleotide consists of a sugar, something called a phosphate group, and one of four **bases** that were nicknamed A, G, T, and C.

At this point, no one knew how DNA was actually put together. Researchers did know that DNA taken from every living thing had the same four bases. Maybe, they thought, it was the way these bases were organized that was the key to DNA's control over inherited traits. Maybe the bases formed a sort of code.

Chromosomes (shown much larger than actual size)

Rosalind Franklin

James Watson and Francis Crick

Assembling the Clues

The race was on to figure out the structure of DNA and break the genetic code. Rosalind Franklin, a young British scientist, provided a vital clue about DNA's structure. She used x-rays to take some "pictures" of DNA.

Those DNA pictures gave American James Watson and Englishman Francis Crick the final piece of information they needed to figure out how the different parts of DNA fit together. In 1953 these two scientists showed that DNA is shaped like a spiral staircase with handrails on either side. The handrails are made up of the sugar and phosphate groups. The bases A, T, C, and G form the stairs.

Actually, each stair consists of two bases, joined together. But not just any two bases—there's a pattern. Base A always pairs with T. Base C always pairs with G. Thousands and thousands of these **base pairs** form the stairs in long, spiraling strands of DNA.

Model of how DNA makes copies of itself

Passing It On

Once scientists knew the structure of DNA, they realized how it passes from one generation to the next. DNA can split down the middle and make copies of itself. Let's see how this works.

When a cell is ready to divide, the long spirals of DNA unwind and the stairs (the base pairs) come apart. Then, the two halves of the staircase separate, like a zipper unzipping.

Next, nucleotides are added to each old half of the staircase so that new stairs are formed. Wherever there's an A on the old half, a nucleotide with a T will pair with it. Wherever there's a C, a G will pair with it, and so on. Stair by stair, a new half of a staircase is built along each old one. When the last nucleotide slips into place, there are two spirals of DNA that are exactly the same as the original one.

When the cell divides, two new cells form, and each of those cells contains a copy of the original DNA. When those cells divide, the same process repeats. With each division, DNA is copied and passed on and on and on.

Base Pairs

A

T

C

G

Cracking the Code

What about the code? How is information about traits carried in DNA? The secret to the genetic code is in the bases, A, T, C, and G. Long strings of these bases contain information used inside cells to make chemicals, mostly **proteins**.

Proteins are the building blocks of cells. Your skin, muscle, and blood cells, for example, are largely made of protein. Your hair and fingernails, like a horse's mane and hooves, are made of protein too.

It's the order, or sequence, of bases along DNA that is the key to what kinds of proteins are manufactured by cells. For example, the sequence A-T-C-C-G-A-A-C-T-A-G might code for one type of protein. A different sequence of bases, C-G-G-G-G-T-A-T-A-G-C-C, would code for a different protein, and so on. These different sequences of bases are separate genes.

At last, the mystery of the genetic code was solved. Sequences of bases make up genes, and each gene contains the instructions for making a particular kind of protein. Inside a cell, those instructions are read and the proteins they call for are assembled. The newly manufactured proteins go into building and maintaining cells— and ultimately—entire organisms.

Thinking Like a Scientist: Collecting and Interpreting Data

Whether you're a detective or a scientist (or both), solving problems involves collecting information and **interpreting data,** or figuring out what the data mean.

No two people, unless they are identical twins, have exactly the same base sequences in their DNA. In the imaginary crime described below, detectives try to figure out who committed a crime. Can you help them?

A masked man tried to steal a painting from an art museum. He was almost caught, but he dropped the painting and escaped. A sharp-eyed detective noticed a tiny piece of skin snagged on the picture frame. The police rounded up three suspects and took samples of their skin. Using high-tech tools, they figured out the sequence of bases in DNA taken from the suspects' skin, and the bit of skin caught on the picture frame.

Their results are shown to the right. Study the data and answer the questions to see if you can solve the crime.

Base Sequence of Skin Clue at Crime Scene
-T-A-T-C-C-T-G-A-G-A-T-A-

Suspect	Skin
1	-C-T-T-A-C-T-A-G-G-G-C-A-
2	-T-A-T-C-C-T-G-A-G-A-T-A-
3	-T-T-A-T-C-T-A-G-C-G-T-A-

Which suspects probably did not steal the painting? How do you know?

Which suspect may have stolen the painting? How do you know?

Would you convict the suspect based on this one clue?

Chapter 3

Secrets of Sequencing

Imagine going to the library to look for a book about codes. To your surprise, the librarian tells you he's pretty sure there are books about codes somewhere in the library. However, he can't tell you where they are. There's no computer catalog to help you either.

Yikes! What a mess that would be. Well, not all that long ago, our understanding of human genes was pretty similar. True, geneticists had cracked the genetic code. They'd identified a few genes, too, and located them on certain chromosomes. However, like a library full of books no one knew much about, our DNA remained largely a mystery. The idea of trying to identify all the genes in the DNA of a living thing—its entire **genome**—seemed an impossible job.

Then in the 1970s, researchers discovered ways to "read" the sequences of bases in DNA more easily. Using high-powered computers, researchers began **sequencing** the genomes of different kinds of organisms. Scientists began with small organisms, such as one-celled bacteria and microscopic worms. Even these tiny creatures had genomes made up of millions of base pairs. But by 1990, scientists were ready to try sequencing the human genome. They wanted to figure out the order of the 3 billion or so pairs of bases that make up our DNA.

Why do you think a genome of a bacterium is smaller than a chicken's genome?

Computers are used to sequence the human genome.

Fruit fly (greatly enlarged and color enhanced)

Genome Sizes
The genome sizes of organisms are measured by the number of their base pairs.

Organism	Base Pairs
E. coli bacterium	4.7 million
Yeast	12 million
Fruit fly	180 million
Chicken	1.2 billion
Human	3 billion

The Human Genome Project

Scientists from many different countries joined in this incredible effort that came to be called the **Human Genome Project** (HGP). The genetic material the researchers used for sequencing was taken from several different people of different races. Using a mix was no problem, because people are 99.9 percent the same genetically.

In June 2000, after 10 years of hard work, researchers with the project reached a huge milestone. They had sequenced enough human DNA to create a "rough draft" of the genome. Not every A, T, C, and G was figured out yet. However, enough base sequences were known for scientists to make some interesting observations.

Craig Venter, President Bill Clinton, and Francis Collins appear at a June 26, 2000, ceremony. They announced the completion of the initial sequencing of the human genome.

Some Surprises

In early 2001, HGP scientists published some of their findings. One big surprise was discovering that humans have only about 30,000 to 35,000 genes. Scientists expected we would have more since humans are large and complex. The exact number won't be known for sure until every base has been sequenced.

Our genes come in different sizes. The average gene seems to be about 3,000 bases long. Some are much bigger. The largest gene sequenced so far contains a whopping 2.4 million bases.

We've apparently got some "junk" in our genome too. That's what HGP scientists are calling base sequences repeated over and over in the genome, which don't code for proteins. No one knows for sure what "junk DNA" does. It may be involved in reshuffling the genome so that over time existing genes are changed and entirely new ones are created.

Figuring out how many genes we have is a huge accomplishment. But many challenges remain. Scientists still don't know where on our chromosomes all our genes are located. Once we know that, however, we'll have a much better idea of where all the "books" are in our cellular "library" of life.

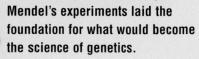

Focus On

Gregor Mendel: The Father of Genetics

One of the first geneticists was Gregor Mendel, a monk who lived in Austria in the 1800s. Mendel performed thousands of experiments on pea plants to try to figure out how certain traits, like seed shape and color, were passed from one generation to the next. Luckily for Mendel, the traits he chose to study happened to be ones controlled by single pairs of genes. Mendel discovered that these traits were inherited in predictable ways. Mendel's experiments laid the foundation for what would become the science of genetics.

Using New Clues

How is knowing the location of every pair of bases in our DNA going to help us? How will figuring out each and every gene—and its location on our chromosomes—change our lives?

One of the most important benefits of this research will be finding out the causes of many inherited diseases and finding a way to cure them. When genes are faulty and fail to do their job, cells—and bodies—don't work properly. The more scientists know about normal genes, the more easily they can spot defective genes and figure out a way to fix them. Fixing faulty genes as a way to treat disease is a fast-growing area of genetics research known as **gene therapy**.

Stay Tuned!

Cystic Fibrosis

Cystic fibrosis is a disease caused by a problem in a single gene. In people with the faulty gene, the mucus-forming cells in their bodies produce thick, gooey mucus. This abnormally thick mucus interferes with breathing and digestion—enough to be life threatening. Doctors are trying to treat cystic fibrosis by replacing defective cells with cells whose nuclei contain a normal version of the faulty gene, so normal mucus is produced. This research may help kids with cystic fibrosis to lead more normal, active lives.

A student builds a model of DNA.

Sequencing the human genome also is a big step toward understanding how DNA and proteins work with each other—and with the environment—to create complex living things. Researchers are discovering the base sequences in the DNA of many organisms. Soon we'll have a much clearer idea of how we are related to the other life-forms with which we share our planet.

However, understanding everything we find in that living library will be up to your generation to figure out. If you think you might want to be a DNA detective when you get older, don't worry. There will still be plenty of mysteries to solve.

Collecting and Interpreting Data

The more we learn about DNA and how genes work, the better we understand the traits that help make us who we are. Collecting information about traits and interpreting what the data mean is a challenging task for geneticists.

Here's your chance to collect and interpret data about a trait that you can smile about.

A single pair of genes controls whether or not you have dimples in your cheeks or the middle of your chin. The form of the gene (allele) that controls having dimples is dominant over the allele for no dimples.

Practice the Skill

Make a table like the one shown below. Do a class survey to find out who has dimples and who does not. Record the results from the survey. (If a person has only one dimple, count the person as having dimples.)

Class Survey for Dimples Trait		
	Number With Dimples	Number Without Dimples
Girls		
Boys		

1. Do you have dimples?
2. How many of your classmates have this trait? How many don't?

Check It Out

What might you conclude about how common the dominant form of the dimple gene is? How could you prove your hypothesis?

Focus On ▶▶▶

Georgia Dunston: Genetics Researcher

Georgia Dunston is acting director of the National Human Genome Center at Howard University in Washington, D.C. She is working to make sure that the information gained about genes from sequencing the human genome is used to help prevent and treat diseases that are common in African Americans. Dunston also started a project that gives Howard University students a chance to participate in human genome research.

DNA Comes Alive!

As you know, DNA makes copies of itself that are passed on from generation to generation. In this activity, you and your classmates will make a person-size "model" of DNA. Then you'll bring your strand of DNA to life by showing the copying process in action.

Explore

1. Divide the class into two equal-size groups: group 1 and group 2. It's best if each group has the same number of students.

2. The students in group 1 (*see photo at left*) should form two lines, side by side. Students in one line should face the front of the room. Students in the

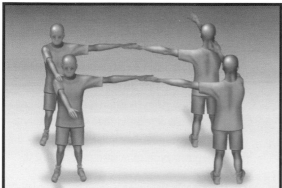

Diagram A

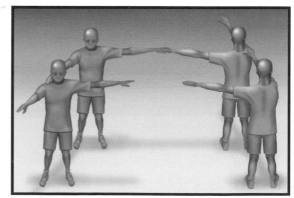

Diagram B

other line should face the back of the room.

3. Next, students in each line should put their right hands on the right shoulder of the person in front of them. With their left hands, students in one line should hold hands with students in the other line. (See diagram A and photo on opposite page.) You've just formed a model of DNA. The extended left hands represent the base pairs.

4. Now, your DNA is going to copy itself. Have the pair of students at the front of the class let go of each other's left hands and step out slightly to the side. (See diagram B.)

5. Now two students from group 2 (red) should move in. Each group 2 student should join hands with a group 1 student (blue). This will start the creation of two new lines. (See diagram C.)

6. Repeat step 4 by having the next pair of students drop their left hands and two new students step in. Continue in this way until all of the students in group 2 have become part of the DNA model. You will end up with two models of DNA where there was one. (See diagram D.)

If your left arm represents a DNA base—part of a step in the DNA spiral staircase—what part of DNA is represented by the arm resting on the shoulder of the person in front of you?

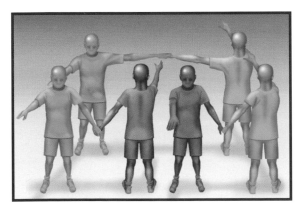

Diagram C

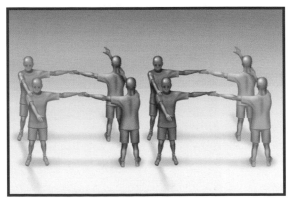

Diagram D

Science Notebook

FUN FACTS

- If you unwound the DNA in one of your cells and stretched it out as a single strand, it would be about 2 meters (6 feet) long.

- If the 3 billion or so base pairs in the human genome were printed as a string of letters such as ACTGCAA . . . the entire sequence would fill 200 telephone-book-size volumes that are each a thousand pages long.

- Certain bacteria have the smallest known genome of all living things—600,000 base pairs.

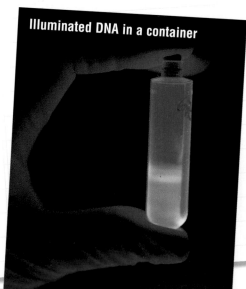
Illuminated DNA in a container

BOOKS TO READ

Balkwill, Fran. *DNA Is Here to Stay.* First Avenue Editions, 1994.

Burnie, David. *Life: Eyewitness Science.* Dorling Kindersley, 1999.

Landa, Norbert, and Patrick A. Baeuerle. *Ingenious Genes* (Microexplorers Series). Barron's, 1998.

WEBSITES TO VISIT

Visit the kid-friendly *Gene Scene* website provided by the American Museum of Natural History: *ology.amnh.org/genetics/index.html*

Use this animated site to learn the basics of DNA, genes, and heredity: *vector.cshl.org/dnaftb/*

Glossary

allele *(uh-LEE-ul)* – a form of a gene

base – one of four chemical building blocks—nicknamed A, T, C, or G—that makes up a nucleotide

base pair – two bases (A-T or C-G) linked to form the "stairs" of DNA

chromosome *(KROH-muh-sohm)* – a long strand of DNA. Genes are found on chromosomes.

DNA – substance in cells that carries information about an organism's traits

dominant – able to override or cover up. In a gene pair, a dominant allele overrides the effects of a recessive allele.

environment – everything around a living thing. Your environment includes the climate, soil, water, food supply, buildings, plants, animals, and people that surround you.

gene *(JEEN)* – a segment of DNA on a chromosome that controls some aspect of how a cell or living thing grows and changes

gene therapy – a fast-growing area of research to find ways to treat, cure, or ultimately prevent disease by changing a person's genes

geneticist *(juh-NET-uh-sust)* – a scientist who studies genes and inherited characteristics

genetics – the study of how characteristics are passed on from parents to their offspring

genome *(JEE-nohm)* – all the genetic instructions for making a living thing

Human Genome Project – an international effort to analyze the DNA of humans

inherit – to receive from one's parents

interpret data – to explain information

nucleotide *(NOO-klee-uh-tide)* – chemical building block that makes up DNA

nucleus *(NOO-klee-us)* – the part of the cell that contains chromosomes

protein – chemical that forms the basic structure of many cell and body parts. Many genes control the production of proteins.

recessive – able to be hidden or covered up. In a gene pair, the effects of a recessive allele will be hidden if a dominant allele is present.

sequencing – reading the base pairs of DNA

trait – a characteristic, such as eye color, that is controlled by genes in a living thing

Index